T0194963

PREACHERS ARE PEOPLE TOO!!

We are not perfect; we have problems
like everyone else

SCHARROD M. WILLS

WestBow
PRESS®
A DIVISION OF THOMAS NELSON
& ZONDERVAN

WestBow Press books may be ordered through booksellers or by contacting:

WestBow Press
A Division of Thomas Nelson & Zondervan
1663 Liberty Drive
Bloomington, IN 47403
www.westbowpress.com
1 (866) 928-1240

Scripture taken from the King James Version of the Bible.

ISBN: 978-1-9736-8206-6 (sc)
ISBN: 978-1-9736-8208-0 (hc)
ISBN: 978-1-9736-8207-3 (e)

Library of Congress Control Number: 2019920663

Print information available on the last page.

WestBow Press rev. date: 01/03/2020

CONTENTS

PREFACE

Preachers have problems just like everyone else. We hurt, we get discourage, we feel alone, we experience fear and we make mistakes. We have problems with our children, our spouse and financial problems. We struggle with the flesh just like other people.

As I began to write down all the facts and problems that does not exempt preachers, it occurred to me that this could be a book.

This book started out as my therapy. I was going through a divorce. Writing everything down enabled me to keep a level head, control myself and also kept me from getting out of character. This made it possible for me to go through the divorce without losing my mind or thinking it was the end of the world. Putting what I was feeling on paper made me realize that Preachers are People Too! Thus, this book and title was born.

A very dear friend told me one morning something that really helped me get through this dark time in my life. He said, "You are not the first one to go through a divorce and you won't be the last. You are not going to die and you will get through this and be alright after it's all over.

After being in the ministry for fourteen years I realized that within those years I had encountered a lot of unexpected difficulties that I never foresaw as being part of the ministry. Being a preacher is not an easy occupation. Most people are only looking from the outside. They only see the glamorous part of ministry. Knowing these things gave me the passion to write this book.

We have problems just like everyone else, we hurt we get discouraged at times, we feel alone, we experience fear, we make mistakes, we have problems with our children, we have problems with our wives. We have financial problems, and we struggle with the flesh just like everyone else. One day as I was writing about the fact that preachers are not exempt from problems, it hit me this can be a book and the perfect name for this book is PREACHERS ARE PEOPLE TOO! Being in ministry for fourteen years at the time this idea came to me I realized that within those years of ministry I had encountered a lot of unexpected difficulties that I never foresaw as being a part if ministry. Being a preacher is not an easy occupation to have, and the funny thing was most people outside looking in did not know it, they only saw the glamorous part of ministry.

This was when the passion to write this book was born.

I believe if you are not really called by God to the ministry, (when problems come your way, and they will come) you will not be able to stand.

To many go into ministry without counting the cost. Most don't realize that there is a cost to be paid, but there is. The cost will bring you face to face with who you really are and let you meet yourself for the first time. Writing this book bought out so many emotions that I had locked behind door and key that I didn't even know that I had. This book also made me deal with "me" and the anger that I was feeling. It ultimately allowed God to cleanse my heart of the darkness that was trying to take hold of me and cloud the way I was thinking. "Praise God." I give Him all the glory and praises for allowing me to write this book, which gave me therapy and the word of God was my peace. Sometimes you have to go through the rain and the storm to get to sunshine.

Life experiences can make you or break you. I chose to let it make me. I try to learn from each of them. Being a preacher's child, I saw what my father went through as an assistant pastor, and as a senior pastor. Some church people "AKA" saint's, can act so unlike children of God. I have seen leaders, preachers, deacons, and ministers forget who they were suppose to be and act totally out of character to the point where they became unrecognizable.

My prayers are that after reading this book you will have more compassion for the men or women who are called by God to preach His word and have the assignment to look out for your soul.

INTRODUCTION

"How beautiful are the feet of them that preach the gospel of peace, and bring glad tidings of good things" (Romans 10:15). Preaching the gospel of Jesus Christ is a great privilege. There's nothing like the feeling of seeing lives changed by the word and power of God. The preachers' job is to bring the good news of The Kingdom of Heaven to the world, and by lifting the spirits of everyone that will listen. Then we all can be elevated by God's word to a higher plain of living. Preaching the word of God is an awesome experience. Seeing God's power and experiencing His presence as He touch those that are willing to receive His touch is a sight to behold.

There are times when Preaching the gospel is not so awesome. The weight of being responsible for souls that God has submitted to your care sometimes seems to choke the life out of you. Some people think that preachers are super human beings. In their eyes, preachers have no feelings and no problems. Many people want to put preachers on pedestals and label them as being perfect but in reality, that is the farthest thing from the truth. Preachers have issues too. There are some preachers that have the mindset that they are perfect and enjoy being put on pedestal.

In this book I will attempt to show the preacher in a light that most people never see. They have problems too. Many times, they are targets to be shot at by the enemy, as well as shot at by the same people that they preach to every Sunday morning. My prayer is that you will look at your pastor, elder, minister, bishop, and evangelist with a little more compassion. Try to understand that the call on their lives is often filled with loneliness and isolation.

I pull from my own experience of being in ministry for over twenty-five years and being in a leadership position at a very early age, to show you that Preachers Are People Too. There are times you want to watch television just like everyone else. Sometime you want to go to the movies and just relax. I'm not saying that anything is wrong with this but most of the time the call will not permit it. The fresh word from God that you need comes at a price. We must pay the price for the fresh word in order for us to give it to you. The discipline, the self -denial, the late nights studying and the early morning prayers are required to get the word to you on Sunday mornings.

I pray after you read this book, you gained a new respect for the man or women of God, and start lifting them up in prayer instead of talking about them when mistakes are made. They need your love and your prayers because Preachers are people too!

THE MIRACLE

As a little boy I had an illness called epilepsy. This disease caused brief lapses of unconsciousness. I would fall and shake all over uncontrollably. Such an attack could last one to three minutes. Once I recovered, I had no memory of the occurrence. It was like dying. All I knew was that I was falling into nothing but darkness. I hated it and I just wanted it to stop. I was around eleven or twelve years old at the time this started happening to me. One day I remember playing basketball at school with my best friend. Suddenly I had an attack right there on the basketball court. When I regained consciousness the teachers where all around me. I had something like a stick in my mouth. I found out later that it was to prevent me from swallowing my tongue. As I think back over those days, I guess I scared my best friend to death. Until now, I never thought of the effect it had on him. I thank God for his friendship. We have been like brothers since the third grade. At age fifty-five I am proud to still call him my friend and my brother. I have learned that true friendship doesn't come easy and they do not come often, so cherish and guard true friendship, never take it for granted.

It got to the point that I was afraid to go outside and play. I was fearful that I would have another seizure. Imagine a little boy scared to go outside and play because he didn't want to have the feeling of dying. What a tough way to live. I loved playing basketball and was pretty good, so I thought, but I never knew when or where I would have another attack. I lived in fear. Always asking myself, "why me? What did I do wrong?" Having seizures affected my mother, sister, and my father. In my opinion we all suffered from this illness that I had encountered. Of course,

I suffered the most. My mother told me much later that the doctors told her to plan my funeral because I would not live long. I was having seizures so frequently the doctors said even if I were to live, I would never be able to go to school and compete with normal children.

To be very honest I would never be normal. He didn't say it like that but that is what he was insinuating.

I remember one Sunday night my mother was reading the Bible to my sister and I. She was reading the story of David and Goliath. She would read the Bible to us every Sunday night. As she read, I began to feel an attack coming on. At age twelve I called it "one of those things". I told mom that I was getting ready to have another one. My mother looked at me with a look that said enough is enough. She said, "Do you believe that God can heal you"? My answer was yes! For some reason I believed that night God could make a house float in the middle of the air. She said I am going to pray. She started praying and so did I. All of a sudden, I was not in my room anymore. I was in this big open space and a thick gray fog was all around me. As I looked up, I saw a ball of fire falling from the sky with a trail of fire behind it. While I looked in amazement that ball of fire landed on the crown of my head. I began to praise God with everything that I had within me. It was awesome! When I came to myself I knew without a shadow of a doubt that I was completely healed.

The next morning my mother told me that she heard a voice say "no more pills, throw the pills away". Mom said she heard the voice twice and she knew it was God speaking to her. But she was hesitant to act on what she heard. When I got up to get ready for school, she asked me if I wanted to take my pills. My reply was, "no more pills, I won't need them anymore". I remember going to school with an awesome sense of God's presence. It was like He was walking right beside me. What an experience for a twelve-year-old boy to have. Glory to God! God is still in the healing business, and I am living proof of that. After this encounter with God my parents took me to see my doctor. My mother, bold in the Spirit, told the doctor what happened to me that night, and how God had healed me. What do you think the look on his face was? Yes, he thought she was crazy! But he smiled and examined me. Mom told him that I stopped taking my medicine and had no signs of the disease. I was not having any more seizures.

After his examination the doctor told my mother, "I will never go against your faith and belief. What I'll do is put his file up and leave it open, if you need us for anything, we will be here with his file ready". He was a good doctor and a caring doctor, but I never saw him again. Glory to God! From this mighty manifestation of God's powers my whole family got saved. We all became aware of God's presence and His love. This started my hunger for the presence and the power of God in my life. From this encounter with God, ministers came forth, my father, my oldest son and me. Years later a church "True Vine Church of Jesus" was started. God had a plan for me and my family. I wanted healing to be a big part of the plan. I could not get the healing out my mind. It has been with me throughout my life. Gods power to heal— Oh how it has changed my life and my family's life.

After God healed me mom and I started attending a Holy Ghost filled church. At this church they were praising God, dancing, shouting, and speaking in tongues. This was a big difference from the church we had attended. Our original ministry had been a blessing too. But God was leading us to this church where the people were, dancing, shouting, falling out in the Spirit, and speaking in tongues. They had drums, tambourines, keyboards, guitars and bass guitars. It was so exciting! There were not just the old people dancing, shouting, and speaking in tongues, but the young people were doing it too. There was a lady minister at this church that was so pretty and elegant. When the Spirit came upon her, she would dance before the Lord with the most delightful dance that I have ever seen. There was another lady there that was a minister. She would become my spiritual mother. She was a very beautiful women of God. She taught me how to study the word of God, and how to search the scriptures and to rightly divide Gods word. When she praised God, she looked like a beautiful peacock strutting across the floor.

The Pastor at this church was a great man of God with a big heart. I remember he had huge hands. When he would pray for me his hands would cover my whole head. There were two young ministers there who were like big brothers to me. They taught me a lot about the word of God.

My greatest teacher other than the Holy Spirit was my father. He has taught me so much about life, ministry, how to be a leader and an ambassador of the Kingdom of God. He has been and always will be my hero!

THE CALL

I have been around preachers all my life. There were and still are preachers in my family. My great, great grandfather was a preacher, Maryland Zollicoffer was his name. He was well known in North Carolina and Virginia. People would walk for miles just to hear him preach. Everyone that is call to the ministry is unique. Grandpa Maryland was no exception. This is how my mother recalls the event. Maryland Zollicoffer was born in Littleton, North Carolina. He was born into slavery. Of course, reading for slaves was prohibited. Going to school was unheard of. But God had a plan. The master had two daughters. Grandpa Maryland was appointed to take them to school and bring them back home. There was a creek they had to cross going to and from school. Grandpa would carry them one by one on his back across the creek to school every day. The girls started teaching him by the creek before going home after school how to read. God had a plan.

At age eighteen Grandpa Maryland was playing baseball with friends. He was a pitcher. He threw a pitch and the catcher threw the ball back to him but the ball was about to speak. He threw the ball again but this time when the ball came back, he heard a voice that said "Maryland Preach". He threw another pitch, and when the ball came back the voice was louder, "Maryland Preach". He threw the third pitch and when the ball came back the voice was even louder, "Maryland Preach"! This time Grandpa Maryland dropped the ball and left the baseball field. So started the ministry of the Reverend Maryland Zollicoffer. He was my great, great grandfather.

My father said that before God called him to the ministry, he found himself preaching everywhere and all the time. He would preach in the shower, in the mirror, in the yard, and driving in the car. He said he felt a burden, a heavy weight on his back until he told God okay.

I had a hunger to see the healing power of God. I read every book I could fine about healing. I heard every sermon I could on the subject of healing. My call to the ministry came as a results of me having dreams about God's power to heal. I would dream of supernatural things happening in my life. I would wake up preaching and feeling the anointing of the Holy Ghost all over me. For example, one night I had a dream I was under a big shaded tree preaching the word of God. There was one man that tried to disrupt what God was doing. It was a large crowd that had gathered to hear what was being preached. The Holy Spirit inside of me became grieved. I said to the man, "you will not be able to walk or see until this message is finished". Immediately he lost his ability to see and he fell down on the ground unable to walk. I preached a very anointed message. The power of God fell on all that was there except the man that sat lame and blind. God allowed him to keep his sense of hearing because he heard everything that took place. After I finished preaching, I turn to the man on the ground and said, "In the name of Jesus rise up, walk and receive your sight. He got up walked and looked right at me and said I want to be saved! Glory to God! My God is an awesome God. I would have dreams like this all the time. I loved it. The anointing was incredible. Under that power there is no limit to what God can do through me. I remember going over to see my mother telling her that God was calling me into the ministry. As I told her tears begin to run down my face. She knew it. She told me to obey God. Little did I know that accepting the call was only the beginning of this journey, there was so much more to learn.

A preacher, Oh, no! Not me! I didn't ask for this it's not a glamour job. I know my father is a preacher. Sometimes he goes through a rough time with the people he is preaching to and praying for. As a young Christian I would see preachers bickering in the pulpit on a power trip trying to be number one. Sometime when Dad would preach other preachers would seat on his preaching. I didn't want any part of that. Me preach, Oh no! God was calling me and I could not run. I knew it was not going to be peaches and cream. I was right it has not been. In my opinion anyone that ask for this job really don't know what they are asking for. Maybe that is the reason God called me because He knew I didn't want it. Hebrews 10:38 says, "God takes no pleasure in them that draw back". The more you say yes, the more God can do with you and through you. I knew if I made myself available to Him everything would work out for me. All I knew for sure was that I had to say yes to God. My life has never been the same. I did not know that the road would be so lonely at times. It's not a glamour job but seeing people saved, delivered, and set free by God's power is worth it all. If you are going to answer the call of God to carry His word, you must have a love for people. You must have a desire to see the will of God done, and not want to see your own will done.

In (Luke 11:2-4) the model prayer some call it the disciple's prayer. It says, "thy kingdom come, thy will be done". If you are going accept this call you have to want His kingdom to come and not yours. I learned that when God call you and you hesitate or ignore His Call, He will just call you again but with a higher volume. You will not be able to turn the volume down it will just get louder and louder until you answer. It is not like He is going to forget there is a call on your life. He is the one doing the calling. He knows how to get your attention. I answered the call and my life has never been the same. There have been highs and there have been lows. One thing has always remained the same, He has never left me, and He has always been there for me.

THE GREAT
MISCONCEPTION

There is a misconception out there that preachers are prefect and that they don't have any problems. They have it all together, they have plenty of money with no worries. Nothing can be farther from the truth. When God picked His disciples He did not pick someone in the palace or a priest in the temple. He choose ordinary men with problems and issues just like you and me. The sad thing is that sometimes preachers get caught up in the hype of thinking that they are perfect. Thinking they are more then what they really are. If people are always telling you how great you are, and how wonderful your sermons are, if you don't give God that glory, you will start taking it for yourself.

Please hear me, you are not great! The God that you serve is the great one. I believe preachers are more of a target for the enemy because of the position that they hold, and the influence that they have for the kingdom. The preacher has problem just like everyone else. They have financial problems, marital problems, problems with their children, problems with their family and of course church problems. People look at preachers and try to put them on pedestals. The sad thing about this is that sometimes the preacher think that he/she should be on a pedestal.

It is easy to get caught up in your own so called greatness. If the enemy can't stop you, he will push you to become full of self. This disqualifies you from being used by God. When this happens you are seeing you, and this will always lead to destruction. Let's look at Lucifer he got caught up in his so called, greatness too. Isaiah 14:12-16, "For thou hast said in thine hear, I Will ascend into heaven, I Will exalt my throne above the stars of God: I Will sit also upon the mount of the congregation, in the sides of the north: I Will ascend above the heights of the clouds; I Will be like the most High. Yet thou shalt be brought down to hell, to the sides of the pit". Notice five times he said "I will" anytime we see our will more than we see Gods will it is a sign of pride and we are headed for the same fall that Lucifer had. God never told us to be great in our own selves but that we could do great things through Him. The error is when we want to be great in self. We are not great. Our God is the great one. He is the one to be worshipped not us. He will share His glory with no one (Isaiah 42:8), that means you!

It is a strange thing that people will tell you that no one is perfect. But those same people will hold the preacher to a standard of perfection that is unfair and unrealistic for anyone to live up to. I am not saying that the preacher or pastor should not be held to a higher standard. The problem comes when people look to the preacher as their example.

The only example the Bible gives us is Jesus Christ. Looking to Jesus as our example will keep the people of God safe. It will prevent the preacher from exalting him or herself. Once again, I am not saying preachers should not be held to a higher standard of living, or that they should not be an example. But I am saying, when we don't meet your perfect expectations understand that we are not perfect, and we make mistakes just like you do. The Bible tells us to honor our pastors and preachers not to worship them. There is a big difference.

Another misconception is that the preacher or minister don't have any feelings. Church folk seem to think they can say whatever they want to say to the preacher and he/she is not suppose to have any feeling about what is said or the way it is said. What planet are you from? How is it that if the pastor forgets to call your name or your visiting friends name in the service you get upset and have an attitude. Preachers are sometimes talked about like they are robots with no feelings. When something is said that you don't like, you are ready to call down fire from heaven and consume the preacher.

The pastor/preacher is supposed to always have a smile on his or her face, never getting upset, always show love even when it is obvious the person expecting the smile is stabbing you in the back. That statement is true, we are supposed to react that way but it does not mean it doesn't hurt. It hurts when people are talking about you and trying to turn the congregations, heart against you. We have feeling just like you. Let me let you in on a secret, in most cases we know who you are that's doing most of the talking, and backbiting. Someone you have talked to have talked to us.

Another misconception is that the Preacher is blind to what is going on. Be warned we see you and know who you are. Just because we smile at you do not mean we don't know who you are. We have to smile and think good thoughts to keep from popping some of you upside the head. I know this do not sound good for a preacher to say but remember "preachers are people too". Some of you have the audacity to look us right in the face and say, "I love you pastor." Knowing what you said and what you have done in an attempt to cause discord among the church. Once again, we smile and say thank you when we know you are just waiting to talk about us behind our back. You stand out like a sore thumb and you don't even know it. The sad thing is sometimes the one doing the talking and backbiting is another preacher. Yes, contrary to what you may think preachers sometimes don't like each other and will show it in their demeanor. You may be saying how can this be? The answer is preachers are people too.

Preachers get jealous, mad, envious, and want to be greater than another preacher in the city. Here we are trying to be greater than one another. Jesus alone is the only true great one. Jesus said in order to be great you must be a servant or to be great in the Kingdom you must serve others. Now that statement destroys what todays church call greatness.

The last misconception I want to mention is greatness of self. The Bible says (Proverbs 16:18) "Pride goeth before destruction, and a haughty spirit before a fall." Pride comes before the fall. We sometimes think greatness is a good thing when in reality greatness of self is a tactic of Satan. He wants us as preachers to try to out great one another by any means possible. If your church is bigger than mine, then I got to build one bigger. Waiting for God to tell me to do it has nothing to do with it at all. After it is built, I will say God told me to do it. If you are driving a BMW then God is telling me to drive one too. Because I am great and He wants me to roll like I'm great. I am a child of the King. I'm supposed to have the best. I agree we are blessed but not if I am trying to out do my brother or my sister with material things. The church has mistaken material wealth for Gods blessing. And that is not true. If material wealth is always a sign of Gods blessing, then the drug dealers are blessed by God. We all know that is not true. We are not in competition with one another. Satan has put blinders on us. We are believing that this competitive nature is of God. It is not of God it is a deception of the enemy.

I have heard preachers say on television, "the bigger the seed you send to my ministry the better your blessing will be." I fully believe in giving but God said give freely not grudgingly because He loves a cheerful giver (2Corinthians 9:7). I know the amount we sow has everything to do with our harvest (2Corinthians

9:6), however; we need to explain that giving to God is what it is all about not necessarily giving money to our ministry. Preachers need to stop manipulating Gods people in an attempt to pad their own pockets. Giving to God means more than just money, it also means giving of one's time. The church needs you and your time not just your money.

Now let me make myself clear so that there is no gray area. The church needs your money. We praise God for your support but don't give out of fear or just because someone tells you to. Give out of love for Jesus Christ. Preachers, let us not add to the misconception of who people think we are. Let's show the world what an ambassador of the Kingdom really looks like.

NOT A
GLAMOUR JOB

When I was in high school back in the eighties it was not cool to say you were going to church on Sunday, going to prayer meeting on Wednesday, or Bible study on Friday night. Saying I love the Lord, talking about how good being saved was and that Jesus was my personal friend was not a cool thing talked about like it is today. I was labeled a church boy. Back then that was not a good label to have, but I didn't care. I was an athlete in school. My sport was basketball. You might say I was kind of popular. I loved looking and talking to the girls. But talking about Jesus was not a way to get dates. I was careful who I talked to about God. I did share my love for Him to many of my friends. Going out on dates was very important to me also. Being seventeen years old I really cared about spending time with the girls too.

I was careful when it came to the girls who I told about the Lord because I wanted to turn the girls on not turn them off. I thank the Lord for His grace and mercy towards me! Being considered a church boy was over looked at times because I was a basketball player, and kind of popular. Praying and talking about Jesus was not as open as it is today. Today saying I love the Lord is okay. Everyone is doing it. When you watch the music awards almost everyone when accepting their award says, "I thank God for this award." Even if what they are saying in their songs is something totally against what God's word stand for. When it comes to some of their music the words in some songs are so disgusting and degrading to women that it makes me cringe. They thank God for letting them receive the award proud of their work, and proud to be recognized. It is popular to say I love Jesus today it helps sells. I'm not saying there is no sincerity to what they are saying, in today's society it is popular to say it. In my day it was not. It is the same way for some Preachers today. A lot of them only see what they consider to be a glamour job. Preaching is perceived by many to be a business opportunity, a way to make money, a way to get notoriety and a lucrative occupation. I want everyone to know it is not that at all. If it is to you then you are doing something wrong. If your ministry is all about you, God did not send you. If the focus is not on Jesus, you sent yourself.

Some ministers have given a false representation of this office. They are living lives of the rich and famous while their congregation is living in poverty. The call of preachers or pastors is not about money or what they have, that is not who God call us to be. Ministry is hard working, dedicated, discipline, and selfless individuals that put Gods people first. What the congregation see is the end result of a sermon, a bible study, or teaching. What they don't see is the work, the prayers, the pain, the missed meals and even tears that go into the sermons and the teachings. The people see the end result of you laying before the Lord. Sometime not understanding yourself, or seeing what God is doing or why He is telling you do something that may seem to be in left field to you at that time. You see, not such a glamour job after all. There are a lot of ministers and pastors that work full time jobs. They still preach, teach, visit the sick, perform funerals, perform wedding, and counsel God's people just like a fulltime preacher does. They do everything that a fulltime minister or pastor would do. Often these ministers receive very little donations or salary for what they do but it is done from the heart. It is their calling. Now let me be very clear there is nothing wrong with ministers and Pastors being full time in the ministry. Praise God that they are able to be in the ministry full time and the church is in the position to have them in full time ministry. But not every minister or Pastor you see are in that position and that is okay too.

If someone is looking at minister thinking this is easy to do, and I can make a lot of money doing this, you need to look again. Full time or not, this is not just a Sunday morning job. It goes far beyond what you see on Sunday morning. If someone is getting into ministry to be praised or to hear people tell you how great you are, this is not for you. Remember that the same people in (Matthew 21:9) that said "Hosanna in the highest" are the same people that was in (Matthew 27:23) that said "let Him Be Crucified!"

Getting into the ministry for the glamour you think it holds, for people to tell you how great you are, and to be considered important by on lookers will not end well at all. The person whose motivation for ministry is this will be in for a big shock! It will be nothing like you think at all.

The singing group, The O-Jays, sang a song that said, "they smile in your face all the time they want to take your place The Back Stabbers". Yes, there are plenty of back stabbers in the church. Ministers and preachers are not exempted from being stabbed or doing the stabbing. Doesn't sound so glamorous after all does it? But this is reality. I just want you to know the truth. More times than I want to admit, the people you help the most are the ones that hurt you the most. You have members in the church that only come to you with nothing but problems, never with encouragement, and never with a solution for the problem. There are many times we may say, "I did not sign up for this". My question is if they did Jesus Christ this way what did you really expect. Jesus never tried to bring attention to himself but deflected that attention to the Father, and so should we. I think that some people look at preachers and pastors as if they are celebrities. They see the multimillion dollar homes, the exotic cars and the one or two jets that they own. This could be seen by some to be living a life style of a celebrity. This is not always the case, there are many pastors that have their own businesses. They write books, put out CD's, and study lessons. Sometimes the media show what they think will sell the most stories. Sometimes what the media is saying is right on point. What hurts the ministry is that there are some that really do think they are celebrities. This can cause people to question the sincerity of the preacher and the ministry. This gives all preachers a bad look and our credibility takes a hit because a few preachers want to be numbered with the rich and famous.

Their life style seemed to be of celebrity status and they roll much like Hollywood movie stars. The scary thing is some of them think they are movie stars. Movie stars for Jesus. Really? Preaching God word is a very sacred assignment to have. It should be viewed as important as the Levites who carried the the ark of the covenant on there shoulders. There was nothing glamorous about what they were doing. It was hard work and they got very little recognition but they were committed to the task. Preaching Gods word is not a glamour job at all!

DEHUMANIZATION

What most people fail to understand is that before the preacher became a preacher, he was a man or she was a woman first. Sadly, there are people who try to dehumanize the man or women of God. In their eyes they are no longer a member of the human race. They are now cybernetic robots from the planet Cybertron. We are supposed to be perfect in every way which is an impossible thing to do. We have no feeling. People can say what they want to say about us and to us. We are not supposed to say anything or have any kind of reaction at all.

Really! The other side of that coin is people try to put us in a worship type position, a sort of God like statue. Again dehumanization. We are not gods to be worshipped. Sometime preachers enjoy and actually seek this kind of praise which just feed into the attitude of robot preacher!

I was talking to a co-worker one night, he was talking about a movie we all had seen. There was a romantic scene and one of the guys ask me how did I look at that scene being a preacher. My answer was "the same way you did, with my eyes". Come on man! How did you think I looked at it? I knew what he was trying to say. I am still a human being and it was a very tasteful scene for that movie. One of the most devastating forms of dehumanization is when the spouse of the preacher or pastor forget their mate is human too. Only seeing the spiritual side and letting the natural side go unattended. This can be a very tragic situation. You see we may have a calling on our lives to preach the word of God but we are still a man or women and still have the needs that a man or women have. The one you love and need the most, the one that you always expect to be in your corner, when they are not there can be very heartbreaking. Preachers and pastors need intimacy too and the spouse need to be aware of that need. Not only are you dealing with the members of the church treating you like you are not human, now your spouse shows you little to no affection, this can be devastating. You already feel isolated by everyone else now you have this isolation in your home, not good!

Being a spouse of a preacher is not easy because of the demands that come with this calling. Please understand that there are two sides to that preacher that must be taken care of, the spiritual side and the natural side. Sometime one or both are neglected. You see a lot of preachers would have you think that they are so spiritual! Yes, they are, but not all the time! I don't know about anyone else but I need my wife to be my wife. Let's keep it real. I want romance, I want excitement and I need intimacy. Everything, that I say I want I also have to be willing to give. Sometime we can be so heavenly minded that we are no earthly good. Fasting and praying is great but if you are always fasting and praying and your marriage is having problems what is God saying to you while you are fasting? I would think somewhere in that fast God would speak to you about your marriage, and what need to be done to make it better. This is speaking to both husband and wife. Please get your head out of the clouds and open your eyes. Preachers have those kinds of feelings, and problems too.

Please understand we don't have the luxury to tell you what is on our mind when someone tries to dehumanize us because there is something on the inside of us that holds it all together. Thank God for the Holy Spirit and the Word of God. But that do not mean that it hurts any less or stops the tears from flowing down our face in the midnight hour. It doesn't stop our heart form breaking. If I had a dollar for every time I had to smile with a broken heart or hurt feeling I would be rich. We may not let you see our feeling but believe me they are there. I would say to the one reading this book, please don't dehumanize your pastor or that preacher that you may know. Remember, they hurt just like you and have feeling just like you.

The hurt is sometimes more severe because they have the compassion of Christ running through their spiritual veins. Instead of saying something they just take the pain. If you are doing the dehumanizing stop it now! You may not have known that you were causing this kind of pain but if you are, now you know, and now there is no excuse!

FAN CLUB

C elebrities and rock stars want and need fan clubs. They want to be admired, worshiped, and adored but Pastors and Preachers should not seek this kind of attention. It will only lead to a big fall. When you start pleasing your fan (people) you stop pleasing your God. Preaching the gospel of Jesus Christ is not something you do to get recognition for yourself. All the recognition should go The Lord Jesus Christ. We do not preach the gospel to get recognition or to become famous. We preach so Jesus Christ can be lifted up and be seen. He is the one that must be seen never us. We have to make sure that the attention is on Him and not on us. In Isaiah 14:12-16 we see Lucifer wanting to be seen and exalted above God. We also see the problem it caused for him that resulted in his fall from heaven.

Wanting to be admired and adored, to be seen above your God, can and will lead to the biggest fall of your life. It is not about us it is about our King. Preaching is not a business. It's not something you do just to get paid. You preach because it's in your heart, its in your spirit, and its in your soul to preach Gods word. You will do it for free because its your work not a job, there is a difference. Dr. Myles Munroe said, "Your job and your work are not the same. Your job is what you were trained to do. Your work is what you were born to do." I was born to preach and preach is what I will do until God see fit to call me home. You see I don't need a fan club telling me how great I am. I know I am only great in the Lord! He gets all the glory, honor and the praise. Its true that some preachers want the attention of fans, they even crave it. Some get caught up in it just like celebrities and rock stars do. So many people are telling them how great they are, and they allow it to get into their spirit. Once its in their spirit its hard to tell them from celebrities. They began to act the same way.

They have to travel with an entourage around them at all times because that is how important they feel they have become. Some say they are their bodyguards, now if the Holy Spirit can't guard your body what make you think that your entourage can? Call me old fashion but come on man!

Like I said, they forget they are preachers and think they are celebrities and you can't tell the difference. They may be talking about the Word of God but even while preaching they are acting like celebrities. It leaves you saying, what are they thinking? What do you think caused Lucifer to fall? He was not created Satan, he was created Lucifer, a beautiful arch angel that covered the very throne of God. His crime was his pride, taking the praise that belonged to God and keeping them for himself, Read Ezekiel 28:12-18. Celebrity minded preachers, after a while of having people praise them, began to think the same way as Hollywood minded people do.

They want to keep the praise and worship for themselves. This leads to one big ugly fall where they are left naked and exposed. Instead of Jesus being lifted up (they just got to be seen) they crave the attention and the spotlight. you see success can be dangerous once you achieved a level of it. You must guard your heart don't let it go to your head. And don't forget who it was that allowed you to get to where you are. Without God none of this would have been possible. This is why preachers do not need or should not seek to have a fan club. You are not a celebrity. You are not a rock star. You are a man or women of God. Make sure Jesus Christ gets all the attention and the spotlight.

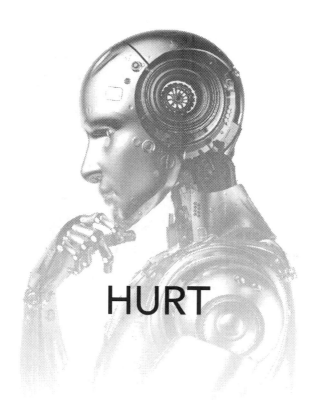

HURT

There has been a lot of hurt that have come with the call to ministry. The same people that said to Jesus "Hosanna; Blessed is He that came in the name of the Lord". Were the same people that just a few days later said "Crucify Him, Crucify Him." The people you help the most are sometimes the ones that hurt you the most. This can make you hard and cause you to put up a wall to protect yourself. In your heart it leaves you empty and can leave you cold. My father and I are very close. We started the church together. He was pastor and I was co-pastor. We shared everything. He preached one Sunday and I preached the other Sunday. We enjoyed working with each other and still do. My oldest son was also called into the ministry. I was a very proud father, my son preaching the word of God. Praise The Lord! He started out playing the drums, he became a really good keyboard player. He became my righthand man. When it came to the music ministry, I really depend on him. When he started playing it took a lot of pressure off of me as far the music was concerned. He was in charge of our young adult ministry. I really relied on him. I just knew he and I were going to be like my father and I preaching the word of God together. I could not have been more wrong! He was going to another church on Friday nights. They were having service for the young people. He really enjoyed the Lord with young people his own age. I thought this was great because he could bring what he was learning there back home to our young people. In my mind I could see how this was going to help the growth of our youth ministry. He did, it was working for a while, but soon I notice on some Sunday mornings he would be setting on the keyboard looking so uninterested in the service. I was not the only one that noticed this. A few members noticed it too. It was like he didn't want to be there. After months of looking at this, one Sunday after service, I asked him what was going on with him. Did he want to go to the church where his friends where. To my surprise he said yes! That hurt me to my heart. Here I was trying to build the ministry that God had given me. My son that I need and depend on wanted to leave and go to a ministry that had everything. Everything he had learned about ministry, the music ministry he learned from us. I felt so alone. I have two boys. They have been in church almost every Sunday since they were babies. In my mind he was a very big part of the ministry. I could not believe he really wanted to leave. But his body language was saying, I want out! At first, I was mad, all that we had poured into him, he learned how to play the drums with us, now he is going to take that talent that we need to another church. He told me about a mentor that he had there that was closer to his age. That did not set well with me. My mentor was my father. You can imagine how that made me feel. To hear that did something to me inside. This is my son telling me he is looking up to someone else as a mentor, I was beyond furious and hurt. I cried like a baby. It hurt me so bad. I had no one to comfort me or say that it would be alright. I made my mind up that day that I would never trust anyone to have my back but God. That day I realized the only one I could ever truly look to be in my corner was God. I let him go. I did my best to show him that everything was okay and that I was alright with his decision. But deep down inside, I was not, I was so crushed!

It was a struggle for me teaching, preaching, playing all the music, and working 60 hours a week. I'm not a fulltime minister but I'm not a part time minister either. That means I work a fulltime job, and minister just as much as a fulltime pastor. I was getting off work on Sunday morning coming to church and having to do what I was depending on him to help me do. It was hard, BUT GOD! God started bringing in people to help with the music ministry. That gave me so must relief. PRAISE THE LORD!

I came to realize that my son was not me, what my dad and I had, we did not have in ministry. I enjoy being around my dad. I love hanging out with my dad.

At that time in my sons' life he did not feel the same way. His vision for ministry and my vision for ministry were totally opposite. One thing that bothered me was he did not come to check on me or the ministry on a regular basis. Once a year maybe he would come to church to see about me. It was always during Pastors anniversary. It wasn't long until my youngest son followed suit and left the church and started going to my oldest son's church or his girl friends church. It was like they forgot that their father and grandfather had a church. I have always been there for my boys. Where were they when I needed them the most? But God had it to be that way because He wanted me to depend totally on Him. He has never let me down!

I have learned not to depend on man but to depend on God. That way if man don't come though I am not hurt or disappointed because I was not depending on man anyway. God was showing me that He was my source not the ones that I had been leaning on.

I had to come to the understanding that God had His own plan for my sons' life. God's plan was not my plan. He knew what He was doing and I had to trust Him.

My son loves the Lord and he was following Gods plan for his life. I am very proud of him and his brother. He is making a difference in the lives of a lot of young people and my youngest son is supporting his big brother. To God be the glory!

We have had ministers that we have helped develop in the ministry. Some have said that before they came to our ministry they thought preaching only consisted of hollowing, jumping, and being emotional. We taught them the difference between preaching and teaching. Giving them opportunity to speak so that they could exercise their gift. Some my father has treated as sons. They all have shown growth in their own personal ministries. We started by allowing them to take turns preaching on some fifth Sundays. All was good, so we thought. Until we found out that some had their own addendum with the group of leaders in the church. It seemed like the more we poured into some and the more we tried to let their gift grow, the more against the ministry they became. It's bad enough to be betrayed by friends and people you work with but when people you are really close to betray you that is a whole new ball game. One of the worst things you can do is to go into business or work with a close friend because that is a hurt, that if not checked, will cause you to go down a dark path of which there may be no return. Let me say this, "don't call me your brother when you are in my face, but when the chips are down and I really need a brother, you are no where to be found." Instead of your support you are the one running me down. If that's what being a brother, I'll pass!

This is a side of ministry that you don't see. We keep it to ourselves. In this book I'm not. You need to know how much PAIN your pastor goes through because of the call that is on his or her life. The hurt is real. The pain is real. Some of it may have even come from some of you reading this book. But its all good because in spite of the hurt we keep moving forward. It's the hurt that helps make us stronger. You know the saying, "What don't kill you, makes you stronger"!

Sometimes you can be hurting form something else, and allow that hurt to blind you. For example,

I have an Aunt that I love very much she have always been like a second mother to me. She has three sons; we were raised up like brother instead of cousins. We were close, and still are Praise the Lord! When I was going through a divorce, I allowed my hurt to drive a wedge between us. I felt like her attention and love was not with me but it was somewhere else. Because of this I pulled away from them and became very angry. I did not know how much I had missed them. I allowed this to lasted for a few years. I even believed that they were all talking about me behind my back. I did not attempt to call them, and they didn't attempt to call me. That is not exactly accurate, the middle son he did call, he tried to get us to bridge this senseless gap that had developed between us. He never stopped calling to check on my father. He stayed in touch. He would eventually become the bridge that would help bring us back together. Let me say this, never get in between a dispute when it comes to family because sooner or later family will come back together, and you will find yourself on the outside looking in. God bought us back together. I realized that I had allowed my hurt to hurt the people that I loved.

Jesus said "judge not so you will not be judged" (Matthew 7:1). He said that because none of us is qualified to judge. We don't have a clue how to judge. Jesus said, "for God sent not his son into the world to condemn the world," now if God did not send Jesus into the world to condemn it what are we doing condemning and judging our brothers and sisters? It amazes me that the people that are living in the glass house are the ones throwing stones. I mean the ones that has the most jacked up lives have the audacity to judge. That is not good!

There were times I wanted to move some furniture around with some people. I felt like the main ones that should have been in my corner were not. Looking back at my storm, I think about Jesus in (Matthew 14:25-31), coming to His disciples walking on the water. Peter asking, "Jesus if it is you let me come out on the water with you. Jesus answer was "come". As long as Peter kept his eyes on Jesus, he was able to walk on the water, but when he took his eyes off Jesus and looked at the storm he began to sink. I was just like Peter I had to realize that all though I was in a storm Jesus was in it with me. As long as I kept my eyes on Him and stayed in His Word, I could walk on the water. Like Peter when I took my eyes off of Jesus I begin to sink.

Let me give you an example. There where some people that I had made up in my mind that I was going to get back for the hurt that they caused me. I had planned what I was going to do to them and how I was going to do it. The more I though about it the closer I came to doing it. I have a good friend that I have known for twenty- two years. She told me something that I felt came straight from God Himself. Her words help me take my eyes off the storm and put them back on God's Word. This is what she said "you are going to be made out to be the villain just don't become the villain". Those words changed my whole mind. I knew that I wasn't the villain but I was beginning to think like one. These words were from The Lord because after hearing them, I didn't want to hurt anyone anymore. It was like all of those thoughts and feeling just disappeared. I never knew my thoughts could be so dark. Praise

God for His word and His people. I am so grateful to my sister in Christ for loving me enough to obey what God was telling her to tell me. It would set me on the course to forgiveness. You never know what you are made of until you are tested. It is in the test that you truly come face to face with you. Oh, how you think you know yourself but when the test come the real you will stand up!

I have learned that God will not trust anyone that He does not test. Jesus was tested in the wilderness in (Matthew 4:1-11). Now if God test His own son, you will be tested too. Who do you think sent Jesus into the wilderness? God did, the Bible says that "then was Jesus led up of the Spirit into the wilderness to be tempted of the devil." Notice doing the test Jesus never came out of character or forgot who He was. Look at how He over came the test. He used the word of God to over come. In the same way He expects us to over come our test using His word. Psalms 119:105 "thy word is a lamp unto my feet and a light unto my path". It was the word of God that kept me from coming out of character and becoming the villain that I was portrayed to be. When you are hurt you can become cold and bitter pushing everyone away, or you can realize this is another learning opportunity to learn more about you.

Storms take you higher and make you stronger. No one have hurt more than our Lord Jesus Christ. Have you ever thought about Jesus having to look and see all the sinful things we say, think, and do? What if you had to look at all the messed up things that your children said and did first hand. I'm talking about murder, hate, lying, cursing, stealing, beating spouse, molesting children, wanting to spend time with everyone else but Him. If that was your child how much hurt, do you think that would cause you? My point is you are not the only one hurting, everyone of us have experience hurt it is how you deal with it that matters. Only God can take the hurt away. Only God can give you true peace of spirit, soul, and mind.

FORGIVENESS

To forgive someone is so powerful because forgiveness is not for them it is for you. The benefits of forgiveness are always for you. As long as you hold on to un-forgiveness that person has control over you. Every time you see that person a chemical reaction inside you starts to take place. You get mad, you want to fight, you want to give them a piece of your mind so bad you can't even think straight. The person that you are mad at is not paying you any mind. They are not thinking about you. They are going on with their life and you are the one stuck in the mud. Mark 11:26 "but if you do not forgive, neither will your Father which is in heaven forgive your trespasses." You see it is very important for you to forgive if you want God to forgive you. We have all done some things in our lives that we need forgiveness for. I have an old friend who I have known for about 25 years. I have told him over and over that he has to forgive people, and stop holding grudges, he has an unforgiving spirit. If you do something to him, he puts you on his list to get you back. Even if the person apologizes to him, that person still has a good chance of getting cursed out. I have witnessed him not accept an apology and still curse the person out.

You know it takes a lot for a person to ask someone to forgive them. They are opening themselves up and putting themselves out there to be forgiven or be rejected. Jesus teaches us to practice forgiveness.

Forgiving is a very hard thing to do sometimes especially if that person has really hurt you. Human nature says no way I am forgiving him/her. But we should not pass judgment or condemn anyone, that is not our job. I know it is so hard to smile and be nice to someone that has tried to destroy you. They may have talked about you like a dog and gone on a personal crusade trying to destroy your character. Maybe they have tried to get into your personal business, in an attempt to create havoc in your life. Here is the crazy part after the dust settles, and things clam down, they come around you like nothing ever happened. In their mind they did nothing wrong. They never apologize for what was done or for all the pain that they caused you. The word of God reminds us to forgive them any way because if you do not you can never move on with your life. You wonder how can a person, especially one that was at one point in time so close to you, do you like that and act like they did nothing at all. What a friend! With friends like that who needs enemies. I heard a message today that really address forgiveness, and un-forgiveness. One of our associate ministers preached about Jonah and how he did not want to go to Nineveh because he didn't want God to forgive the Ninevites. Now we want forgiveness but there are people that we don't want to forgive and don't want God to forgive either.

I had to remind myself that even if someone did me wrong the God that I serve still loves them just as much as He loves me. With that in mind forgiveness is a must, you have to let it go. Now I'm not saying that you have to go out to dinner with them or hang around together, but you do have to forgive them and not hold a grudge. God can not bless you through un-forgiveness. You have done something in your life before that you wanted God to forgive you for too. Here is a key you need to remember you are not perfect and you make mistakes. You have to come to a place where you are at peace with yourself because the one person that you are around everyday is you. In (John 3:16) it says, "God so loved the world that He gave His only begotten son." Notice it did not say God so loved the church. That means that God loved the world so much He gave His only son Jesus Christ. If God love the world, we as people of God should love the world too. We don't have to agree with the life style of the people in the world but we have to love them, meaning not judging them but loving them. Forgiveness means putting yourself last and considering the one you are forgiving first. God is love and He has a heart full of forgiveness.

Galatians 4:4-7 tells us that God sent Jesus Christ to redeem us from under the curse of the law. We can now receive the adoption as one of His sons. God forgiving us made us something much greater than what we were before "sons of God" not servants. He died for sons not servants. Now think about the power of forgiveness that you can unleash on your enemy, or that person that just tried to destroy you. God would not allow them to to destroy you. Your willingness to forgive has just changed the direction in which you were going. Remember forgiveness is for you not for the person that you are forgiving. You can never move forward living in the past. This is why so many people are trapped in time they are unwilling to forgive. Your stress level will be better if you learn to forgive. That blood pressure would not be an issue practicing the art of forgiveness.

This is so good for your spirit, soul and body. Forgiveness shows the love of God in your life. Only love can truly forgive. 1 Peter 4:8 says, "love covers a multitude of sins" love will compel you to forgive even when you don't feel like doing it. God is your father and He is love, so you can display His love in your life and in your heart just like him. If you find yourself not forgiving you need to ask yourself this question, "Is God really my father, is He really Lord of my life?" We are always saying that we want to be more like Jesus Christ. Then What Would Jesus Do? You know what He would do, He would forgive. If the king says forgive, we must forgive. In a Kingdom the word of the king is law, and as citizens of the Kingdom of Heaven our culture is to forgive that is what we do. This keeps us healthy and in perfect alignment with God. I'm not saying it is easy but God knows it is absolutely necessary if we want Gods best for our life. God cannot and will not bless you when you are in un-forgiveness. Understand it dose not matter what they did or how they did it. God is concerned about your response, because that is what you have control over. The way you respond to difficulty is what God is looking at. How will you conduct yourself in the face of trails, and problems? This is a trial of your faith. If He is God of your life then let Him Be God. Trust in Him and believe that He will bring you out like He always has, victoriously. I am a witness that He will show up and show out. Don't allow anger and your pride to keep you away from the victory God has for you. Practice the art of love. Let your motivation be filled with love. Let your desire be to show love. If you give love and show love it will come back to you. Maybe not from the person that you are showing it to but it will come back. In (2Corinthians 2:5-11) Paul states to reaffirm our love for God we must forgive. We must practice the art of love. He also says in verse 11 that one of the devices, schemes or weapons of Satan is to get us to have an unforgiving heart because it works against us and work in his favor. At one time in my life I worked as a pipefitter on submarines and aircraft carriers putting piping systems together. I had to braze fitting to go on the pipes. The copper brazing ring inside the fitting connected the pipe and fitting together. Once I had the pipe and fitting prepared, I would take a brazing torch and start heating the fitting with the pipe inside until the copper ring began to melt and flow out making a beautiful shiny seal connecting the pipe to the fitting. Once the system was completely fabricated, I had to do an air test and a water test to see if the connecting parts were good and leak free. Now think of un-forgiveness as trash in the system, once water is introduced to it, if there is trash in the pipes it will greatly restrict the flow of water and if there is enough trash in the pipes it will stop the flow of water altogether. Paul said let us not be ignorant of the weapon of Satan. Un-forgiveness will clog up your system stopping the flow of Gods blessing to your life.

Let me explain, the purpose of the water test we will call this the trials of your faith. It is to test for leaks and cracks in your life. After the brazing is done and the pipe and fittings are cleaned, it looks great, the copper pipe is shining the fittings and the ring that connects the two is beautiful shining sliver. Everything looks great. It's perfect but once the water test starts and the pounds per square inch is increased it fine all of the pin holes that the naked eye could not see. It will find all of the flaws that did not appear to the eye. This is the reason for the test and this is why you must not allow un-forgiveness to clog up your life. The system is your life. The fitting is your character. God is perfecting your character so you can look just like Him. It is amazing that you really do not know what you are made of until the trials of life come your way. During the trials, you find out where you are strong and where you are weak. James 1:2-3 says, "count it all joy when different trials come because it brings patience into our life," Once your faith has been tried with no trash restricting the flow of Gods blessing then you can add to your faith virtue which means power (2 Peter 1:5). Remember when the woman touched the hem or border of Jesus' garment He said that virtue which is power was pulled out of Him (Luke 8:42-47). As you can plainly see the trials of our faith and the perfecting of our character causes the power of God to flow through us, bless us and the people we come in contact with. Why would you let that power be restricted because you are not willing to practice the art of love through forgiveness? Life can take you through some rough times no one is exempt from the storms of life. Sometimes you are going to get wet, cold, hot, time of exultation, time of abasement, be loved, be hated, mistreated, falsely accused, and just be in the wrong. Forgiveness and practicing the art of love, the love of God is the only way to get through to the other side of your storm. I know I've been there.

DIVORCE

D ivorce is a traumatic experience. The word traumatic means emotionally disturbing or distressing. Everyone at some point in life has been involved in some kind of relationship that has failed from kindergarten on up to adulthood. Some of those broken relationships left scars or even sores that have not healed. Traumas cause distress, and distress manifests in anxiety. When you began to be anxious, quite often you become somewhat irrational. Being irrational mean you begin to act without thinking properly.

If your arms were torn away from your body, there would be tremendous pain. Secondly, there would be a loss. Forever after, your nervous system feels as if something is still there. Yet, you are aware that it is gone. Such are the after effects of a broken relationship or divorce. Of course, there is always healing. Even after amputation, there is healing.

Immediately after a divorce is not a good time to make major decisions, and certainly not a good time to get involved with someone else. Your wounds are still tender, if not bleeding. If you marry a person that is wounded they are tender. If you touch them the wrong way, they cry out. Marrying on the rebound just sets you up for another traumatic experience.

I don't think anyone that is serious about marriage go into it expecting it to end in divorce. I do feel that marriage can be entered into not fully understanding what is expected. Men and women are different. The definition of love to a woman is not the same to a man. For example, (Ephesians 5:25) it tells the man, "Husbands, love your wives, even as Christ also loved the church, and gave himself for it; That he might sanctify and cleanse it with the washing of water by the word. That he might present it to himself a glorious church, not having spot or wrinkle, or any such thing; but that it should be holy and without blemish." But notice in verse 33 of Ephesians it tells the wife to "Reverence her husband." The Bible tells the husband to love his wife but for the wife to reverence her husband.

Why do you think it tells the women to reverence her husband and not tell her to love her husband? First let see what the definition of the word reverence is: the word reverence means – a feeling or attitude of deep respect. I believe the reason that God stated it this way is because men interprets respect as love. Talking positively about him to other people, praying for him, praying with him. These are just a few examples of respect. Sisters I am not saying you are not supposed to love your husband. I'm just speaking on the way God worded it. The word submit in the Bible sometime can be a problem between husband and wife, because it can be viewed as a word of domination. Before we go any further let's look at (Genesis 1:26) it says, "and God said, let us make man in our image, after our likeness; and let them have dominion over the fish of the sea, and over the foul of the air, and over the cattle, and over all the earth and over every creeping thing that creepeth upon the earth."

Notice he did not give man dominion over man. That means man do not have dominion over woman because she is man also. The species that God created was man, but man comes in two models male and female. Gods plan was for them to rule together. With this understanding and looking at the content in which the word submit is used. Let's look at (Ephesians 5:22-24), "wives, submit yourselves unto your own husband, as unto the Lord, For the husband is the head of the wife, even as Christ is the head of the church; and he is the savior of the body. Therefore, as the church is subject unto Christ, so let the wives be to their own husband in everything." Now let me put your mind at peace about the word submit. If your husband is treating you like Christ treats the church then wives you should have no problem submitting yourselves to your own husband. On the other hand, my brothers if you are not caring for your wife like Christ cares and treat His church, then you should not expect her to submit herself unto you because you are not worthy of it. Wives I'm not leaving you out, if your husband is treating you like Christ would treat His church, and you are not respecting, submitting to him, you are not worthy of him. If the husband is not treating you like Christ would treat His church, wives if he is, and you are not respecting and submitting to him, both of you are sinning before God. Marriage only works when you work it, and is willing to fight for it when it is going in the wrong direction.

After saying all of this I know sometimes it just doesn't work out. You grow apart if certain aspects of marriage go unattended. I believe anything that is important to you, you will spend time with it or doing it. If you are not spending time with it or doing it then it really is not that important to you. This is true with your spouse and it is true with God. If you are not spending time with God, I don't care how much you say you love Him, He is really not that important to you.

Going back to divorce, I once heard a minister say that divorce was worse than death. When someone dies there is funeral service, everyone has a chance to say goodbye, the body is put in the ground and you never see them again. When someone get a divorce and the service is over, I'm talking about the courtroom service, no one is put in the ground. There is a very good chance that you may see that person in the Walmart, in Target, in Food Lion, that person just keeps popping up, and those feeling whatever feelings you are having keep being resurrected. When I first heard this, it was so hilarious to me, but after giving it further thought, it is an excellent observation to what divorce does to a person. Until you are able to deal with the different feeling surrounding the divorce it can feel like the dead coming back to life.

Regardless of who is at fault, most times both parties played a part in the death of the marriage vows. Divorce signifies the fatality of the marriage and the death of what should have been. It is a reflection like no other. The person that was suppose to be your lifetime partner decides I want out of this union. You and this marriage is not worth fighting for. I know of people who received divorce papers that felt exactly that way, not saying that they did everything right but sending divorce papers was not an option that they were considering. When they received the divorce papers it turned their world upside down. A divorced person experiences the loss and the humiliation every time they check the "single" or "divorced" box on any form. Divorce can become an identity. Don't let that happen to you. It was an event not your identity. God still sees you as His precious child one purchased by His blood. Divorce is not a death sentence. I have a good friend that made this statement about divorce, he said, "you are not the first one to go through a divorce, you will not be the last one, you are not going to die, its not the end of the world, you will get through this, and you will be just fine after it is all over." Very encouraging words when you feel like your world is crumbling down all around you. Remember God still loves you. He still loves both of you. He is a mender of broken hearts.

I feel the church can do a better job in equipping those that want to get married by helping them understand what they are getting into. By explaining the responsibility of the husband and the wife in this union. Everyone did not come from the same back ground, everyone was not raised the same. Some had parents that showed love and affection and the children came up seeing that. So, to show that kind of affection when they get married is normal for them. Some came from a family where the parents showed very little affection to one another. When they get married showing little to no affection is normal for them. You are a product of your environment. What you see and what you are around becomes embedded in your DNA, unless you are willing to say to yourself the way I was bought up and what I saw as normal was not normal at all. An affectionate person and a person that shows little to no affection will have a very difficult time in a marriage union. I believe when the church has a marriage seminary, and when a couple is receiving counseling for marriage, any and every subject regarding marriage should be put on the table for discussion. Getting pass the feelings of infatuation, receiving the knowledge and responsibilities of marriage some may decide to pump the breaks and reevaluate this marriage thing. What you see on television is not reality. Being married takes work if it is going to be successful. Have you ever heard that marriage is supposed to be

50/50? I don't agree with that anymore. I used too. If marriage is 50/50 than each person is only half a person. If this is true you have two half whole people, and this is a problem because they will spend the rest of their lives trying to steal from each other in an attempt to get what is needed to become whole and that is not good.

Let's look at the history of divorce to see where it came from and what God has to say about it. In (Matthew 5:31) it begins with Jesus saying,

"It hath been said, whosoever shall put away his wife, let him give her a writing of divorcement."

Who said this? The Jewish people whom Jesus was teaching in the Sermon on the Mount knew what Jesus meant. He was referring to the writings of Moses in Deuteronomy.

"When a man hath taken a wife, and married her, and it come to pass that she find no favour in his eyes (is not pleasing him), because he hath found some uncleanness in her: then let him write her a bill of divorcement, and give it in her hand, and send her out of his house"(Deuteronomy 24:1).

Moses was protecting women with this bill of divorcement because in Moses day the men were leaving their wives for "any other reason". The any other reason was other than the sin of adultery. Moses did not mention adultery as a condition for divorce, because there was only one consequence of adultery: death by stoning. That is why the Pharisees asked Jesus if it was lawful for a man to put away his wife for every cause (Matthew 19:3).

The men could repeat three times, "I divorce you" and leave their wives to marry someone else. However, the wives could not remarry without a legal paper, bill of divorcement. Many times, they did not have any means of support when their husbands left. Moses was setting forth a process the men had to go though to get rid of their wives: 1) Write her a bill of divorcement. 2) Give it to her. 3) Send her away.

The phrase "send her away" is a figure of speech used from the time the Israelites were "sent away" by the Egyptians. It meant to send someone off with goods, money, and so forth. When a master freed a slave, he was to "send them away" with certain things: a certain amount of money, an extra suit of clothes, and some cattle. In other words, anyone "sent away" was to have enough to start life over again. Jesus was saying, "Moses command your ancestors to give wives a writ of divorce because their hearts were hardened and they were leaving their wives destitute with out hope for another marriage. But I say it is not lawful in the sight of God to leave your wives for every cause in the first place. Furthermore, I have come to bring mercy, so instead of stoning a woman caught in adultery, divorce. And that is the only cause for divorce – the breaking of the marriage vows not every little thing she does that you do not like."

Then Jesus pointed out that what Moses had allowed, God had never intended. God made male and female and joined them, the intent was for a man to leave his parents and cleave to (be glued to, chase after, or be united with) his wife. God said not to let anyone separate the couple bonded together by vows. Divorce is not Gods perfect will. He hates divorce but He will not let that define who you are or will it stop Him from loving you. His love, His mercy, His grace, His blood is greater divorce. If God will not let it define you don't you let it define you either. People have asked me how is life after divorce, my answer is "its different".

Let me close this chapter with this statement: Marriage is what you make of it. Please don't take each other for granted. What you did to get one another that's what you need to do to keep each other. Communicate with one another, go places together, spend time with each other, have date nights, pray together, laugh together, don't give up without a fight, and that means both fighting for it to work.

My prayer is that you will never have to go through a divorce. I pray your marriage stays strong, healthy, and blessed. But if you do happen to go though a divorce know this, it will not define who you are. It will not stop you from being used by God. If it happens use it as a tool, learn from it, and keep it moving.

God Bless!

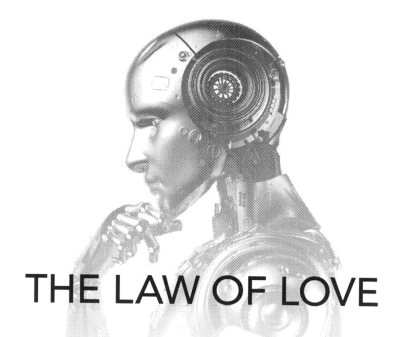

THE LAW OF LOVE

G od don't love like we do; Gods love has no emotions or feeling attached to it. His love is based on His commitment to loving us. Emotions are actually chemical reactions in your brain. The problem with chemicals is they change quite often, and are never stable. If your love is based on emotions and feelings your relationships will be unstable just like chemicals. Love is a choice you make. Your will to love not feel to love. This is where the problem comes in, instead of choice we feel and when the feeling is gone so is the love. That is not true love. Most of what we call love is nothing but infatuation. The definition of infatuation is "an intense but short-lived passion or admiration for someone or something". It is not Agape love that divine love that God has. I think we experience a sample of agape love with our children. Think about it, you love your child regardless of how they act or what they do. Our love for them is that of commitment and not based on emotion and feeling. If our love for our children was based on feeling and emotions, we would not put up with what they do, it would be like I'm done. All that agree say Praise the Lord!!!

The art of love is to learn how to love with no emotions or feeling attached to it. Strictly a choice and an act of your will. When this happens, you can look pass a person faults and see need. You can love an unlovable person because now your love is based on their need and not on your needs.

What is love? Love is a decision to commit to meet the needs of another person without expectation. Love is unselfish, it is patient, love is kind. When you truly love someone, it is not all about you its more about the other person. Love is anticipating a need and meeting it right now or before the person ask for it.

There are four Greek words of love in the Bible:

1. Philieo – is brotherly love.
2. Eros – is Erotic or fleshly love.
3. Storge – is friendship mutual love.
4. Agape – divine Godly love.

PHILEO: is a companionable love this love speaks of affection, fondness or liking someone a love that comes out of one's heart as a response to the pleasure one takes in a person or object. Phileo is a love that responses to kindness, appreciation, or love, it involves giving as well as receiving but when it is greatly strained it can collapse in a crisis. Phileo is a higher love than eros because it is our happiness rather than my happiness this love is called out of one's heart by qualities in another.

EROS: this is an erotic love an arousing or satisfying sexual desire, a love of passion an overmastering passion that seizes and absorbs itself into the mind.

It is a love that is an emotional involvement based on body chemistry. The basic idea of this love is self-satisfaction though Eros is directed towards another it actually has self in mind for example "I love you because you made me happy."

STORGE: This love has its basis in one's nature. Storge is a natural affection or natural obligation. It is a natural movement of the soul for husband, wife, child or dog. It is a quiet abiding feeling within a man/woman that rests on something close to him/her and that he/she feels good about.

AGAPE: is called out of one's heart by the preciousness of the object loved. It is a love of esteem of evaluation. It has the idea of prizing, it is the noblest word for love in the Greek language. Agape is not kindled by the merit or worth of it's object but it originates in it's own God-given nature. God is love. This love delights in giving this love keeps on loving even when the loved one is unresponsive, unkind, unlovable, and unworthy it is unconditional love, agape desires only the good of the one loved it is a consuming passion for the well-being of others.

Let's take a look at the love chapter in the Bible to see what God has to say about love that we as kingdom citizens suppose to have: (1Corinthians13) says, "everything we do must be motivated by love if not we should not do it because if love isn't in it that means God is not in it."

Let me give you an example of the art of law. I have a friend who has a sister who he loves very dearly. She was diagnosed with breast cancer. You could imagine it came as a shock and tears begin to fall. As a Pastor his first though was trust in God which was her thought process also. After she got herself together and could think clearly, she began to develop a plan. She was a member of his church but she was not attending as a faithful member at the time. There were some things that happened in her personal life that she allowed to keep her away from her home church. She would attend other churches from time to time, his thought was to leave her alone it would work itself out, and she would be back in her own sweet time.

That did not happen. She just stopped coming all together. He missed her and wanted to encourage her not to let anything or anyone keep her away from her home church. Now he really wanted her back in church. He decided to encourage her to go to one of his friend's church. She needed to be feed and if she felt she could not be feed at her home church he knew she needed to eat Gods word somewhere. She went to his church and really enjoyed herself. She started going from time to time and begin to receive from that ministry. He was really unhappy about it inside but tried to remember the Art of Love and that it was not about him, it was about her and her needs not his. This was going good for him for a while; did you hear that "for him." Until he felt lead to tell her that she needed to get the elders of the church to pray for her according to (James 5:14-15) which say "is any sick among you? Let him call for the elders of the church; and let them pray over him, anointing him with oil in the name of the Lord and the prayer of faith shall save the sick and the Lord shall raise him up and if he hath committed sins, they shall be forgiven him". Alright this would get her back in the church who else would pray for her but him and the elders of her home church. Oh, yea, she getting ready to come back home was his thinking. Well it didn't work out that way she still wasn't comfortable about coming to her home church to get prayed for. When he heard that it stopped being about her and it started to be about him. How could she not want to come to her home church and receive prayer from the elders. He said to himself, she needs to forget what she thinks people will say and get what she needs from the Lord with me.

Once again, he was thinking about Himself. You are probably saying what did she do to keep her from her home church. the answer is nothing. It's what someone did to her by someone that wasn't a member of the church. But it was done in kind of an open way in her home church, and she may have felt some kind of way about it. What he felt she didn't see she had a great deal of support form everyone at her home church. He was a little hurt but trying to practice the Art of Love he suggested that she go to his friend's church and get the elders to pray for her. It was not about what he needed but what she needed. She did it reluctantly and it was all good, however; he started getting a bad feeling about everything because only one person prayed for her and elders mean elders more than one person. Plus, he felt like it should have been him praying for her. Once again thinking about himself. He stopped calling her for a while because he did not want her to pick up on how hurt he was. Well that only caused her to suspect that there was something wrong with him because he called her at least one to two times a week. He said he wasn't going to pray for her because she needed to be somewhere, and with someone she was comfortable with. When they did talk, they had a little argument for the first time in their lives. After they fussed as grandma would say he remembered the message on the art of love that I had preached. He said my love must be without feeling or emotions attached to it. This is not about me its about my sister getting what she needed to go though this trying time in her life. He had to be her biggest supporter so what he did was call her and said I wanted our elders to come and pray for you. He did not know that this is what she wanted all the time. She just didn't want to be prayed for at the church, she was so happy. He had to get over it being about him because the Love that God wants us to display is all about the person you are loving and not about you. They got together anointed her with oil according to scripture and oh how God blessed her. She started speaking in tongues like a river was flowing out of her. It was like the Holy Spirit inside of her was just waiting to pray on her behalf it was beautiful. You see we can no longer love with our feeling and emotions we must learn how to love with our will, our commitment and leave feelings outside. Only the love of God can love in spite of someone's faults, only the love of God will allow you to detach your feelings and emotions so you can put that person first and give what they truly need. That is unconditional love. Practice the Art of Love it will change your life.

CLOSING WORDS

M y prayer is that this book has cast some
insight into the life of ministry, especially
the life of the preacher. We are not perfect and we
do not have it all together but we serve a God who
is perfect and has it all together. We should never
carry ourselves in a way where we are holier than
every one else because we are not. My personal life
went through a lot of changes while writing this
book. In writing my hurt and pain down on paper it
has been healing for me. I was able to put words on
paper and convey my heart. I want to make it clear

I have no ill feeling against anyone that may have took me through a rough time. I still pray for and ask God to bless everyone because I don't have time to hold negative thoughts, and bad feelings inside my heart. I most likely cause pain and heartache too. The only thing I want to fester and grow in my heart is love and not my love but the love of God. If God could love me so much until He sent Jesus His son to die for me, before I came into this world then I can love to. Please remember this if you don't remember anything else in this book, God holds us accountable for three things:

1. What we say.
2. What we do.
3. What we think.

These three are truly the only things we really have control over.

I close this book with a prayer:

Father thank you for your grace and your mercy. Thank you for Jesus and the blood that he shed for our sins. Because of the blood we have access to everything in the Kingdom of Heaven. Because of the blood we have the fullness of the Holy Spirit, because of the blood we can love your way. Dear Father I ask a special blessing upon every reader, bless them with divine health, bless them with divine prosperity, bless their family, and help them to understand that Preachers Are People Too. Cause them to pray and lift them up to you for protection and guidance. Knit our hearts together in love. Help us to make a difference for the Kingdom of Heaven, in Jesus Name Amen!